A day in the life of

Anna the nurse

Monica Hughes

Heinemann
LIBRARY

Little Nippers

www.heinemann.co.uk/library
Visit our website to find out more information about **Heinemann Library** books.

To order:
Phone 44 (0) 1865 888066
Send a fax to 44 (0) 1865 314091
Visit the Heinemann Bookshop at www.heinemann.co.uk/library to browse our catalogue and order online.

First published in Great Britain by Heinemann Library, Halley Court, Jordan Hill, Oxford OX2 8EJ, part of Harcourt Education.
Heinemann is a registered trademark of Harcourt Education Ltd.

Editorial: Jilly Attwood and Claire Throp
Design: Jo Hinton-Malivoire and bigtop, Bicester, UK
Models made by: Jo Brooker
Picture Research: Catherine Bevan
Production: Lorraine Warner

Originated by Dot Gradations
Printed and bound in China by South China Printing Company

ISBN 0 431 16523 8 (hardback)
06 05 04 03 02
10 9 8 7 6 5 4 3 2 1

ISBN 0 431 16528 9 (paperback)
06 05 04 03 02
10 9 8 7 6 5 4 3 2 1

British Library Cataloguing in Publication Data
Hughes, Monica
A day in the life of a nurse
610.7'3069
A full catalogue record for this book is available from the British Library.

Acknowledgements
The publishers would like to thank the following for permission to reproduce photographs:
All photos by Tudor Photography.

Cover photograph reproduced with permission of Tudor Photography.

Special thanks to Anna Smith and the staff at the Horton General Hospital, Banbury.

The publishers would like to thank Annie Davy for her assistance in the preparation of this book.

Every effort has been made to contact copyright holders of any material reproduced in this book. Any omissions will be rectified in subsequent printings if notice is given to the publishers.

Contents

Meet Anna the nurse

This is Nurse Anna.

Nurse Anna works at this hospital.

Before work

Anna gets Daniel out of bed.

She then eats breakfast
with her family.

The day starts

Anna changes into her uniform at work.

Doctor Charles

The first patient

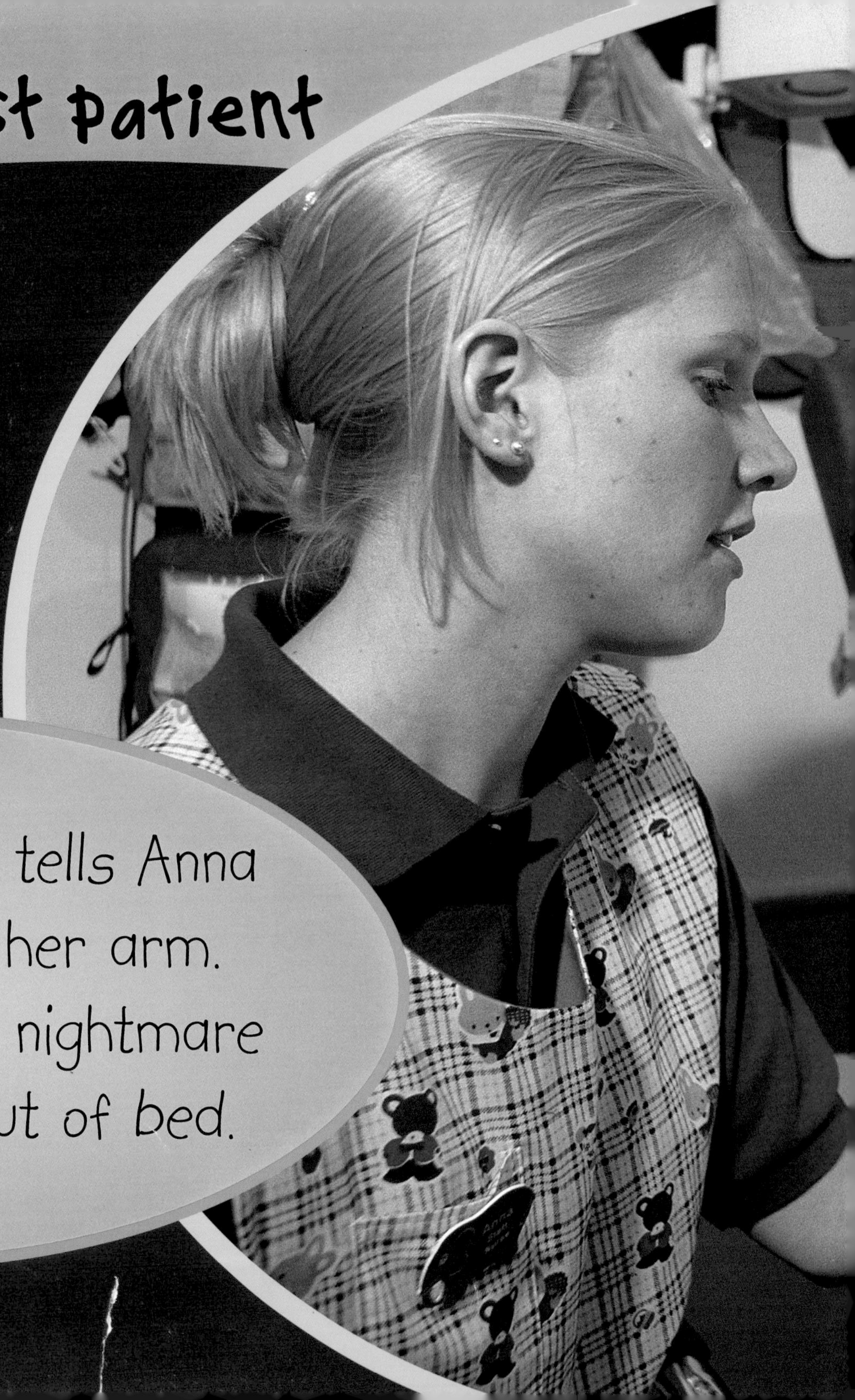

Mary-Ann tells Anna she hurt her arm. She had a nightmare and fell out of bed.

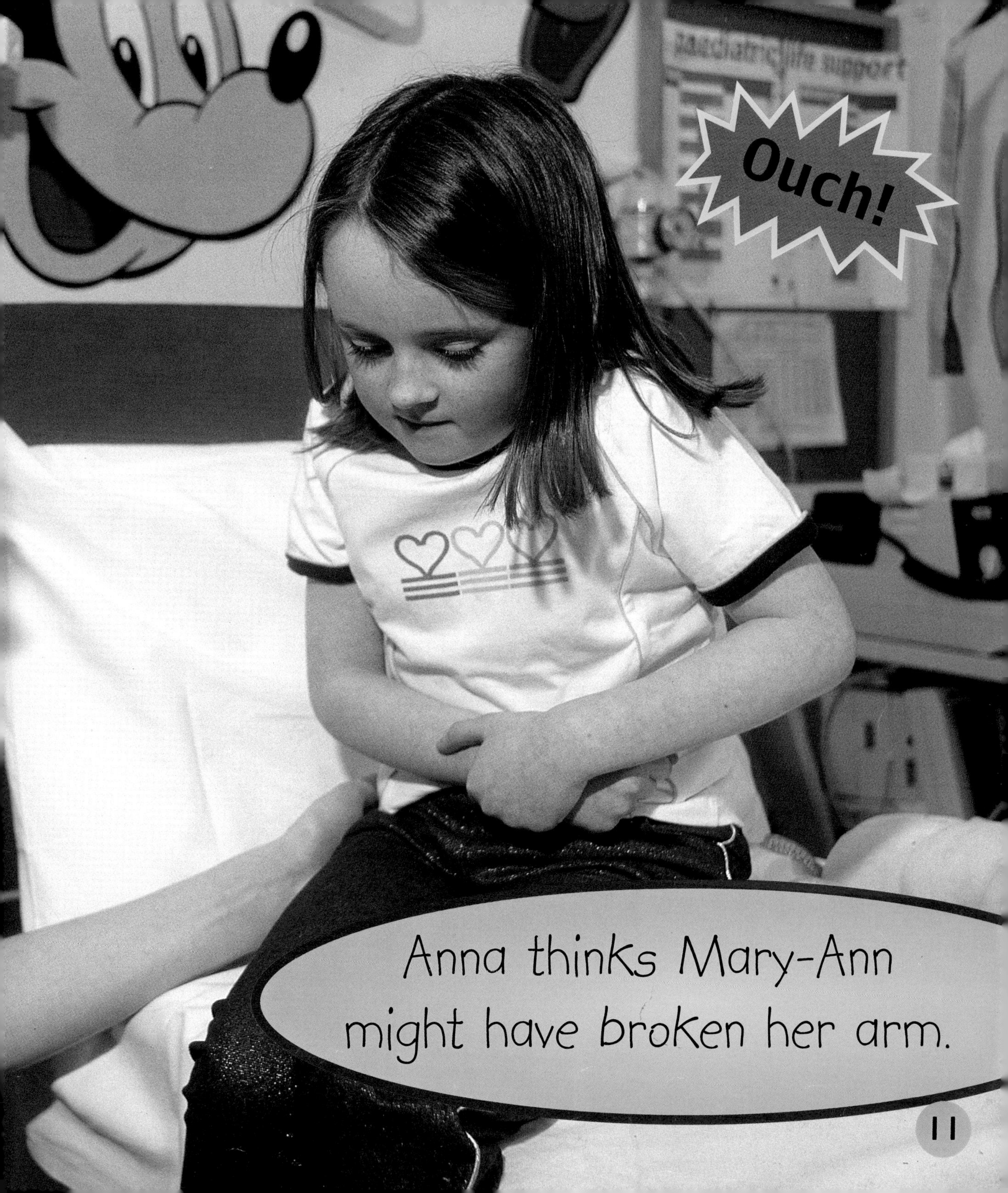

Anna thinks Mary-Ann might have broken her arm.

An X-ray

Anna shows Mary-Ann the X-ray of her arm. It's not broken.

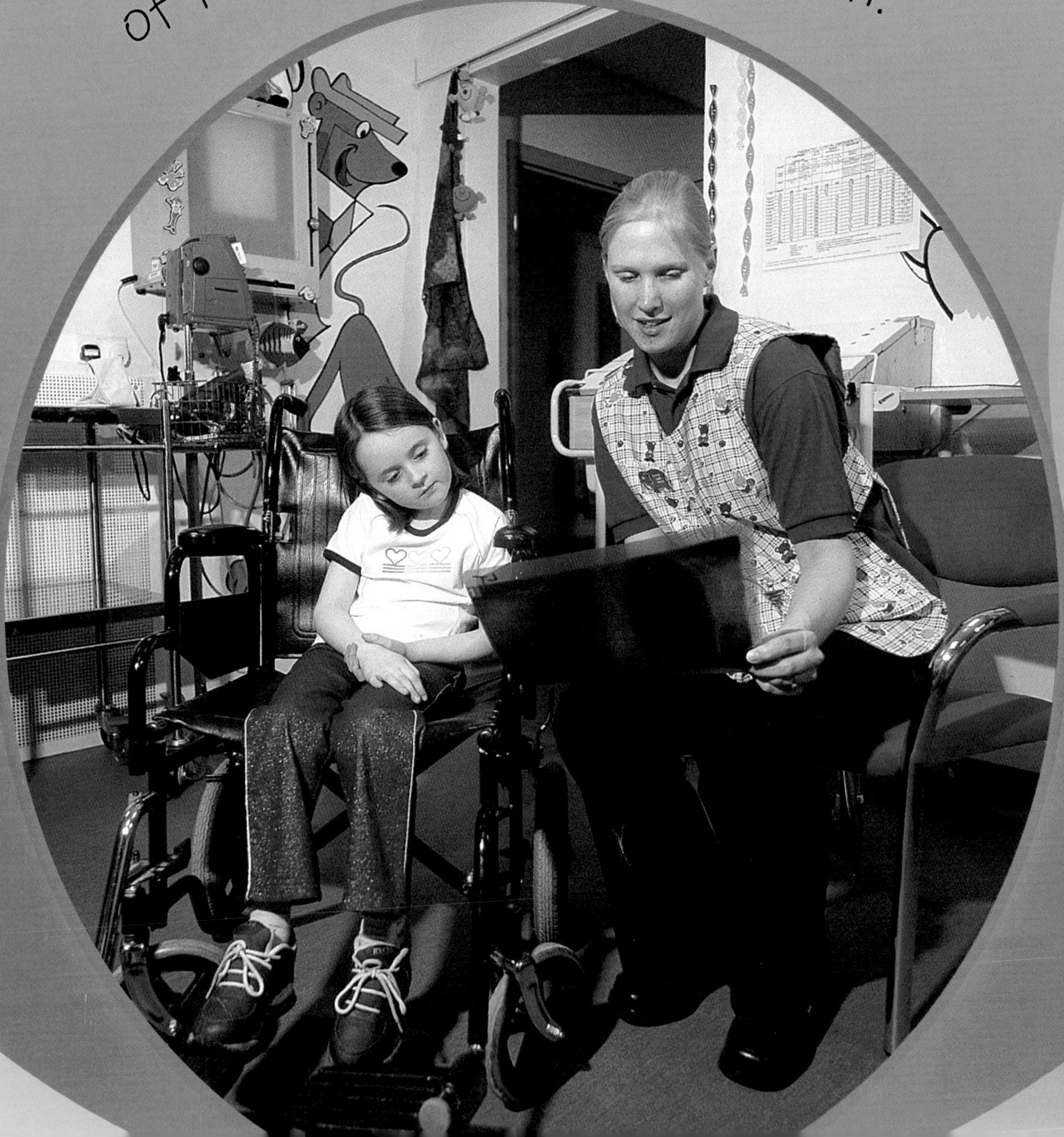

Anna puts Mary-Ann's arm into a sling.

More Patients

Anna takes the temperature of a boy who is not feeling well.

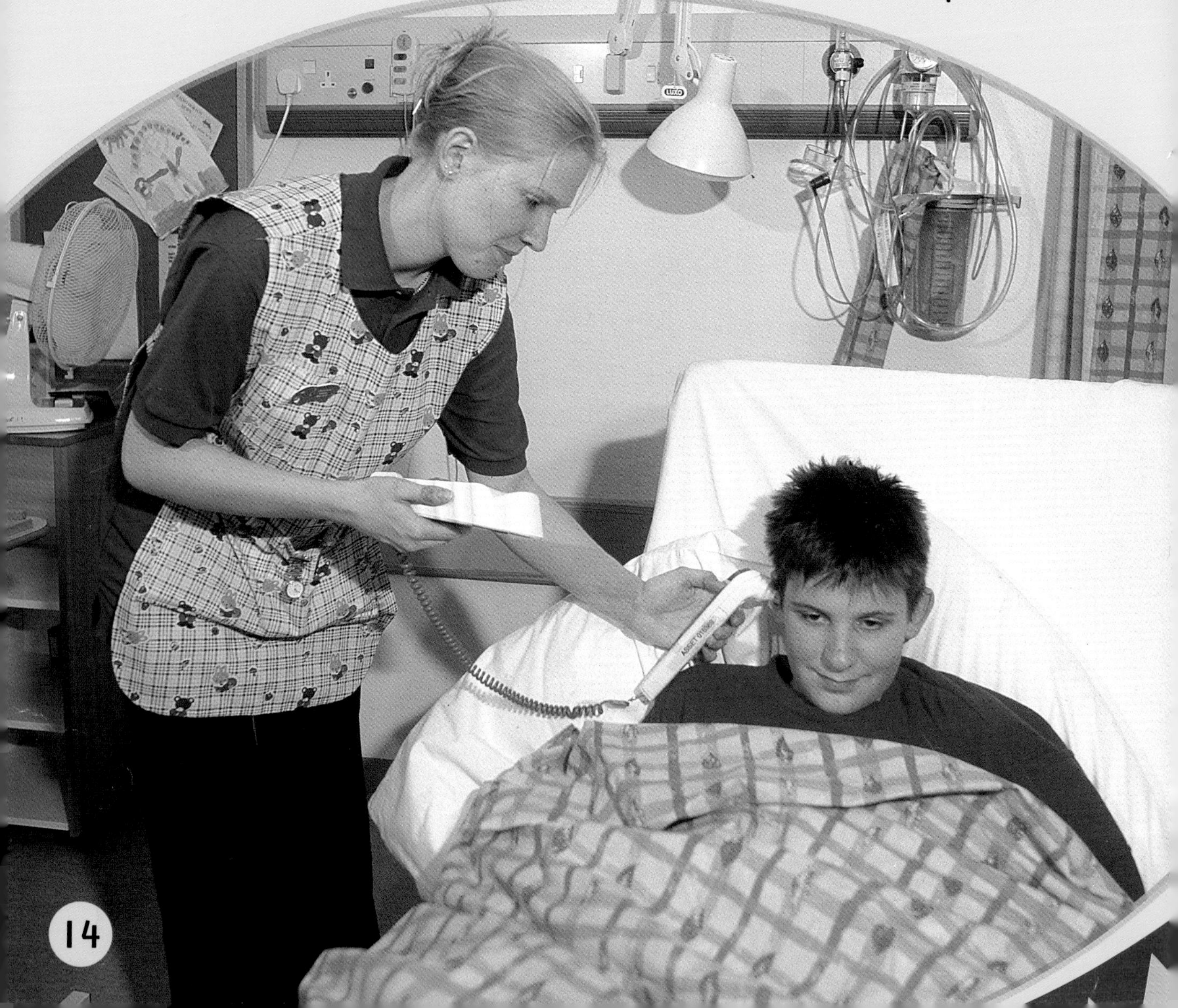

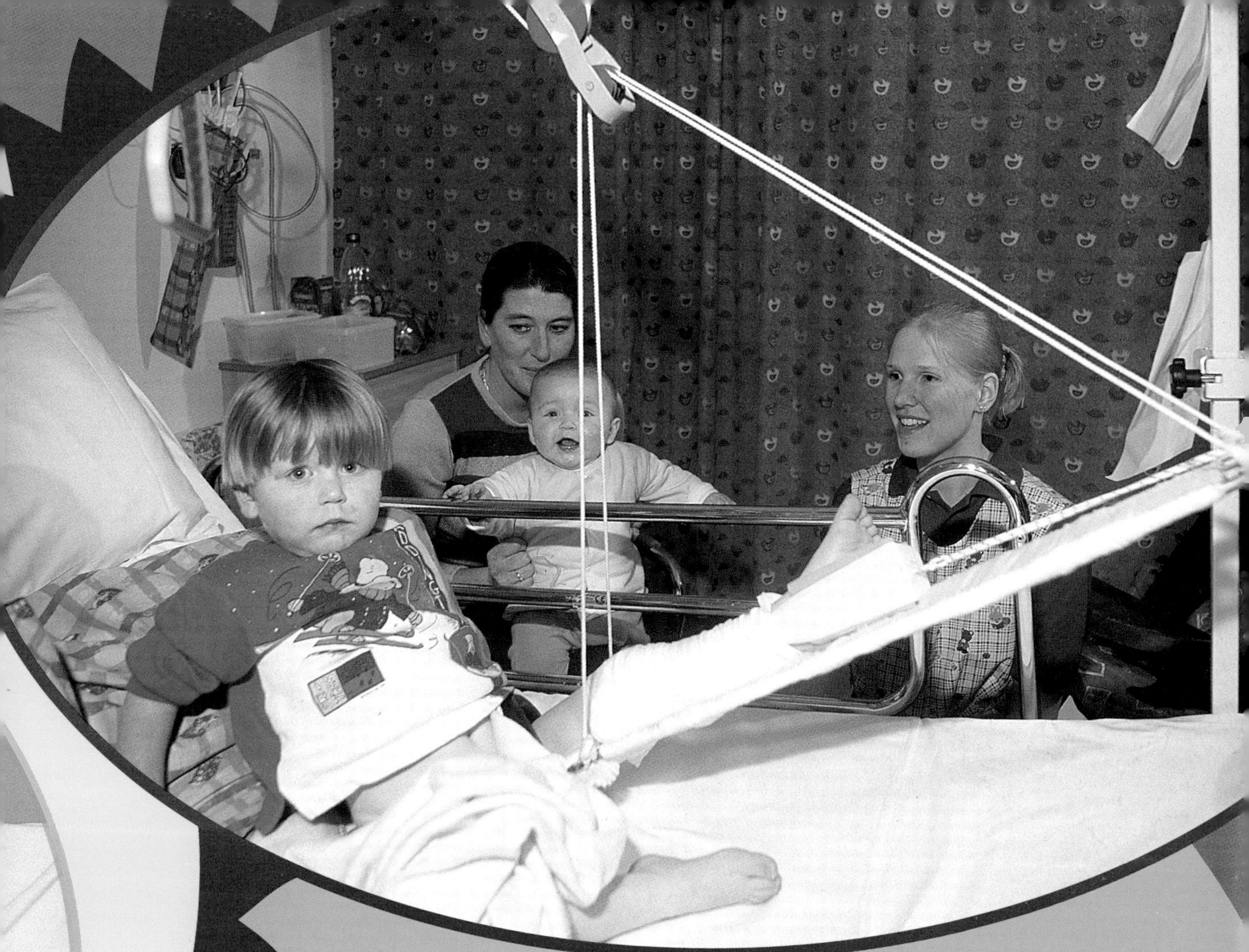

She talks to the parent
of a little boy who has
broken his leg.

Breaktime

It is very busy in
the children's room.

An emergency

Anna talks to a new patient and listens to her chest.

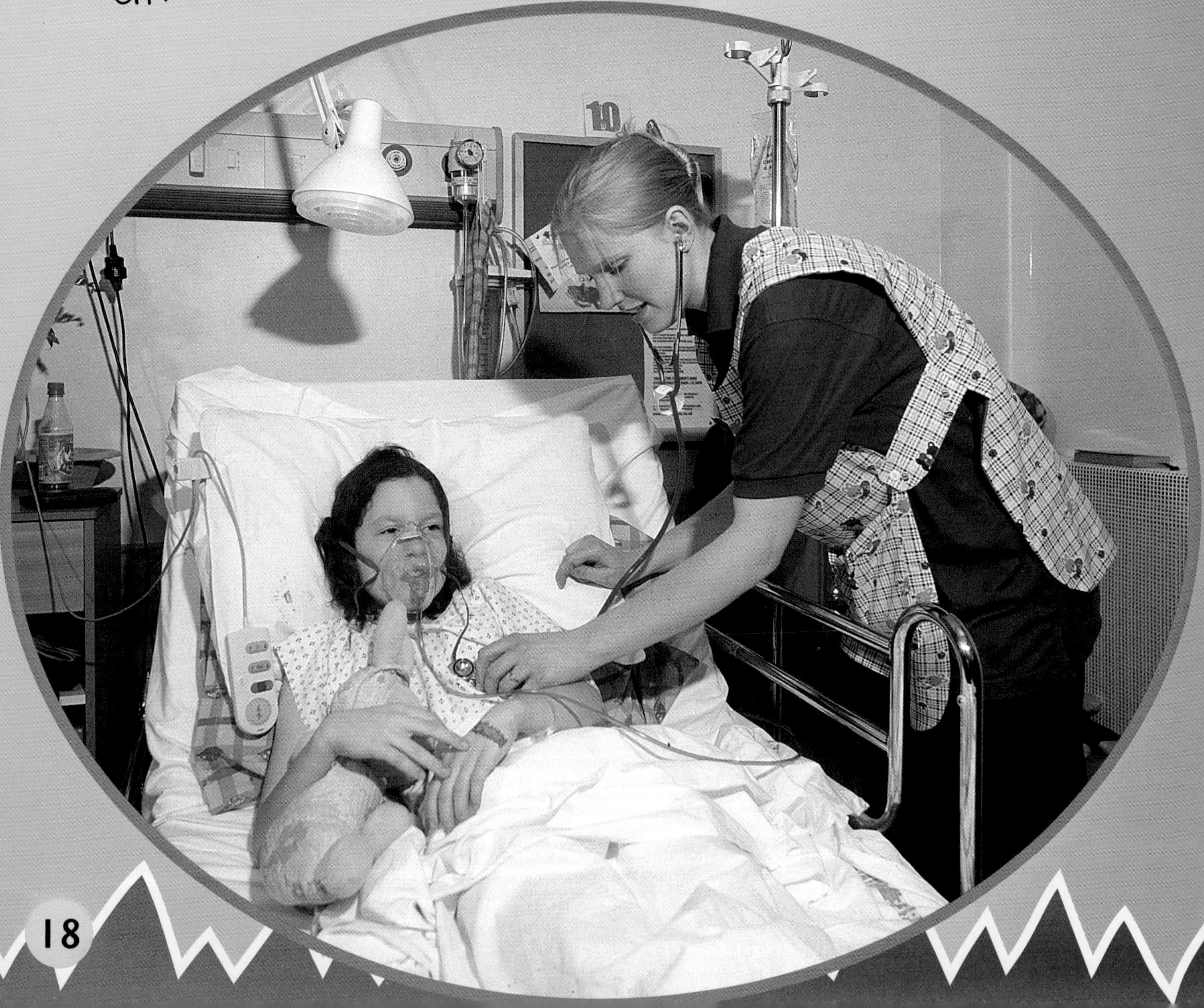

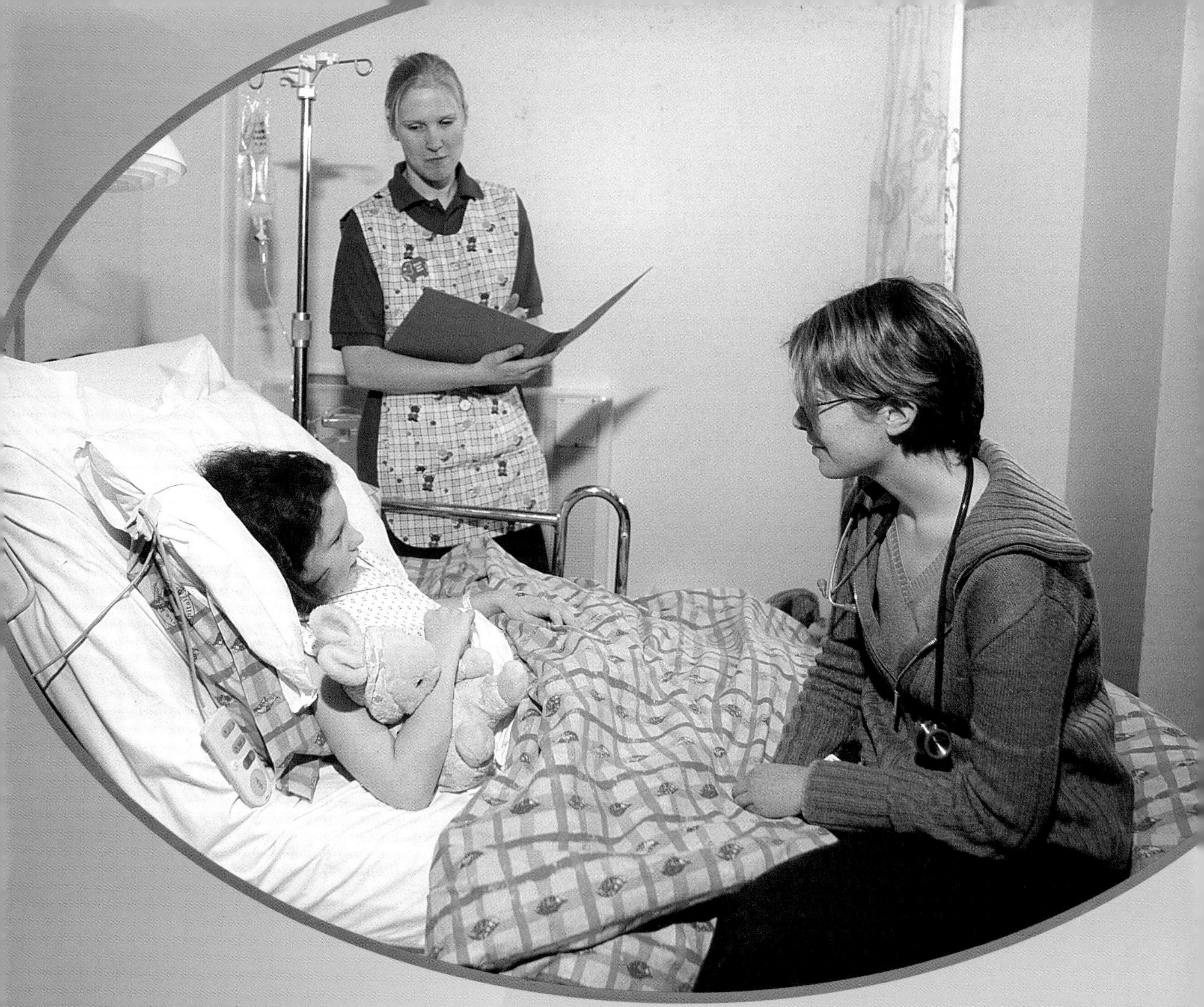

Doctor Tanya examines the patient and says she has to stay in hospital. Have you ever stayed in a hospital?

Looking after the patient

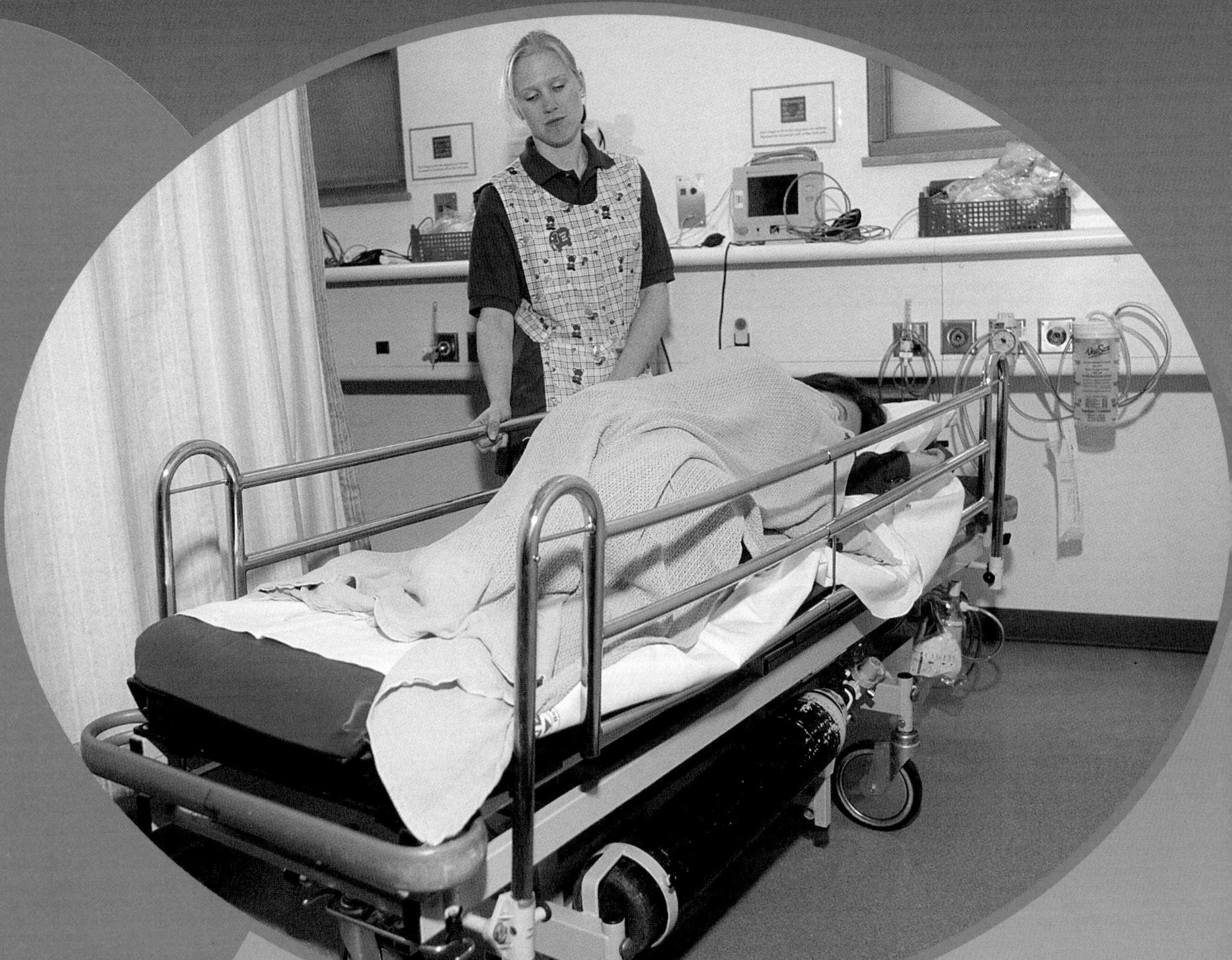

Anna goes with the patient to the children's ward.

Finally it is time
for Anna to go home.

The day ends

Anna gets home from work and relaxes with her family.

Then she goes to sleep.

Index

Notes for adults

This series supports the young child's exploration of their learning environment and their knowledge and understanding of their world. The following Early Learning Goals are relevant to the series:

- Respond to significant experiences, showing a range of feelings when appropriate.
- Find out about events that they observe.
- Ask questions about why things happen and how things work.
- Find out about and identify the uses of everyday technology to support their learning.

The series shows the different jobs four professionals do and provides opportunities to compare and contrast them. The books show that like everyone else, including young children, they get up in the morning, go to bed at night, break for meals, and have families, pets and a life outside their work.

The books will help the child to extend their vocabulary, as they will hear new words. Some of the words that may be new to them in **A Day in the Life of a Nurse** are *hospital, patient, nightmare, X-ray, sling, temperature, examines* and *ward*. Since words are used in context in the book this should enable the young child to gradually incorporate them into their own vocabulary.

The following additional information may be of interest:
On the ward the nurse is responsible for the day-to-day care of patients and works in partnership with the doctor. She also offers support and advice to the patient's family. A broken limb may be made immobile by the use of a sling or traction.

Follow-up activities
The child could role play situations in a hospital ward. Areas could be set up to create a ward and a nurses' station. The child could also record what they have found out by drawing, painting or tape recording their experiences.